i can't believe i'm CROSS STITCHING

Everything You Need to Know.

I always get excited when my Editor-in-Chief asks me to put together a new title in this series, because of all the many people who've written to let me know that their first exposure to their greatest passion began with the purchase of one of these publications.

Welcome to **I Can't Believe I'm Cross Stitching**. Cross stitch is one of the oldest forms of needlework, and you'll find examples in many of the world's folk museums. Yet, despite its great age, cross stitch remains very popular with today's stitchers. I think that popularity is because it is so very easy to do.

Simply put, cross stitch is no more than stitching Xs onto fabric to create a picture. Backstitch is added for definition, Quarter Stitches to create curves, and French Knots and Lazy Daisy Stitches for special interest. The technical term for this form of needlework is counted cross stitch, because the stitcher counts the squares on the chart and then counts the same number of squares on the blank piece of fabric to determine where and how to stitch. In the world of needlework, however, it has become commonplace to refer to this form of stitchery as simply cross stitch.

In **I Can't Believe I'm Cross Stitching**, we tell you everything you need to know and then some—how to choose your fabric, needles, and floss, how to read charts and color keys—even step-by-step instructions for Leisure Arts' exclusive Stitch 'n Paint and Stamp 'n Stitch techniques! Our detailed and easy-to-understand instructions, hints and tips, quick reference page, and specially-developed designs make it easy to perfect your cross stitching skills.

But be warned: I've never met anyone who told me that they **used** to cross stitch.

Deb Moore
Craft Publications Director

TABLE OF CONTENTS

LEISURE ARTS, INC.
LITTLE ROCK, ARKANSAS

FABRIC

CHOOSING FABRIC:

CROSS STITCH FABRICS COME IN MANY DIFFERENT COLORS AND FABRIC COUNTS. THE HIGHER THE COUNT, THE SMALLER THE FINISHED DESIGN WILL BE. OUR CROSS STITCH CHARTS LIST THE FINISHED SIZE OF THE DESIGN FOR DIFFERENT FABRIC COUNTS.

■ **14 COUNT AIDA** IS ONE OF THE MOST POPULAR AND IS EXCELLENT FOR BEGINNERS. AIDA IS THE FABRIC TYPE AND **14** REFERS TO THE COUNT (THE NUMBER OF SQUARES PER INCH).

■ **PREPARING THE FABRIC:** BEFORE CUTTING THE FABRIC, ADD AT LEAST SIX INCHES TO THE DESIGN SIZE TO ALLOW ROOM FOR FRAMING OR FINISHING. KEEP THE EDGES FROM FRAYING BY ZIGZAGGING AROUND THE EDGES OR USING A FRAY PREVENTATIVE.

FLOSS: EMBROIDERY FLOSS IS AVAILABLE IN DIFFERENT COLORS AND BRANDS. EACH COLOR IS IDENTIFIED BY A NUMBER THAT VARIES BY BRAND. IF YOUR PATTERN CALLS FOR A BRAND OF FLOSS NOT AVAILABLE IN YOUR AREA, CONVERSION CHARTS—WHICH GIVE THE CLOSEST COLOR SUBSTITUTION IN ANOTHER BRAND—ARE AVAILABLE ON THE INTERNET.

STRANDS: EMBROIDERY FLOSS CONSISTS OF SIX STRANDS OF THREAD TWISTED TOGETHER. THE NUMBER OF STRANDS YOU WILL USE DEPENDS ON THE COUNT OF YOUR FABRIC. OUR CHARTS TELL YOU HOW MANY STRANDS TO USE FOR THE BEST COVERAGE. AFTER CUTTING A LENGTH OF FLOSS, SEPARATE THE STRANDS, AND THEN REALIGN THE CORRECT NUMBER OF STRANDS BEFORE THREADING THE NEEDLE.

NEEDLES: CROSS STITCH IS WORKED WITH TAPESTRY NEEDLES. THE BLUNT TIPS ALLOW THE NEEDLES TO SLIP EASILY THROUGH THE HOLES IN THE FABRIC, AND THE LARGE EYES MAKE IT EASIER TO THREAD SEVERAL STRANDS OF FLOSS. LOOK FOR TAPESTRY NEEDLES IN SIZE 24 OR 26 (THE LARGER THE NUMBER, THE THINNER THE NEEDLE).

WHAT'S IN YOUR SUPPLY STASH? SUPPLIES

HOOPS: CROSS STITCH CAN BE WORKED WITH OR WITHOUT A HOOP. USING A HOOP HELPS KEEP THE FABRIC TAUT, MAKING IT EASIER TO PUT THE NEEDLE IN THE FABRIC HOLES AND CREATING NEATER STITCHES. HOOPS COME IN A VARIETY OF SHAPES AND SIZES AND ARE MADE FROM MANY DIFFERENT MATERIALS. SOME STITCHERS PREFER SIMPLY HOLDING THE FABRIC. CHOOSE THE OPTION THAT IS MOST COMFORTABLE FOR YOU.

CHARTS & KEYS

■ CHART: EACH CROSS STITCH DESIGN HAS A CHART WITH A GRID SIMILAR TO GRAPH PAPER. EACH SQUARE ON THE CHART REPRESENTS A SQUARE ON THE FABRIC. A STITCH IS WORKED ON THE FABRIC FOR EACH SYMBOL SHOWN ON THE CHART. THE SYMBOLS IN THE CHART CORRESPOND TO THE COLOR KEY, WHICH INDICATES THE FLOSS COLOR FOR EACH STITCH.

ARROWS: ■
CHARTS HAVE ARROWS TO HELP YOU LOCATE THE CENTER OF THE DESIGN SO YOU CAN CENTER IT ON THE FABRIC.

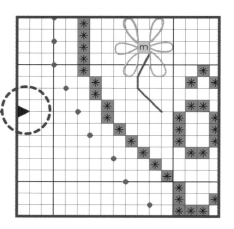

■ COLOR KEYS: COLOR KEYS INDICATE THE FLOSS COLOR AND TYPE OF STITCH USED.

LOVE

X	DMC	¼X	¾X	B'ST	ANC.	COLOR
m	444				290	yellow
♥	606	◩	◩	◪	334	red
	907			◪	255	green
✳	3845				1089	blue
●	606				334	red French Knot
⬭	970				316	orange Lazy Daisy

X — THIS COLUMN SHOWS A SYMBOL WHICH SHOULD BE WORKED AS A FULL CROSS STITCH.

DMC — THESE NUMBERS INDICATE THE FLOSS COLOR TO USE IF YOU'RE USING DMC BRAND FLOSS.

¼X — SHOWN IN A TRIANGLE, EACH OF THESE SYMBOLS SHOULD BE WORKED AS A QUARTER STITCH. THESE STITCHES ARE USED TO CREATE CURVES IN THE DESIGN.

¾X — SHOWN IN A TRIANGLE, EACH OF THESE SYMBOLS SHOULD BE WORKED AS A THREE-QUARTER STITCH. THESE STITCHES ARE USED TO CREATE CURVES AND FILL IN SPACES NEXT TO THE BACKSTITCH.

B'ST — THESE STRAIGHT LINES SHOULD BE WORKED AS BACKSTITCH. THESE STITCHES ARE USED TO OUTLINE AND DEFINE PORTIONS OF THE DESIGN.

ANC. — THESE NUMBERS INDICATE WHICH ANCHOR BRAND EMBROIDERY FLOSS COLOR TO USE.

COLOR — THIS IS THE NAME GIVEN TO THE FLOSS COLOR.

■ DESIGN INFORMATION: THE DESIGN INFORMATION SPECIFIES THE STITCH COUNT, COLOR, AND TYPE OF FABRIC USED FOR THE PHOTOGRAPHY MODEL, AS WELL AS THE NUMBER OF FLOSS STRANDS USED. NOTICE THAT THE DESIGN SIZE IN OUR EXAMPLE IS 2" x 2¼", BUT THE MODEL WAS STITCHED ON AN 8" X 8¼" FABRIC PIECE. THIS REFLECTS SIX INCHES ADDED FOR FRAMING OR FINISHING.

Love was stitched on an 8" x 8¼" piece of 14 count White Aida (design size 2" x 2¼"). Three strands of floss were used for Cross Stitch, two strands for Lazy Daisy Stitches, and one strand for Backstitch and French Knots.

Stitch Count (28w x 30h)

14 count	2"	x 2¼"
16 count	1¾"	x 2"
18 count	1½"	x 1¾"

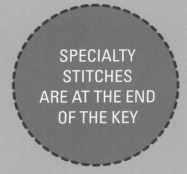

FRENCH KNOT — A LARGE DOT LISTED NEAR THE END OF THE KEY SHOULD BE WORKED AS A FRENCH KNOT.

LAZY DAISY — AN OVAL LISTED NEAR THE END OF THE KEY SHOULD BE WORKED AS A LAZY DAISY STITCH. THE CHART WILL INDICATE THE EXACT SIZE AND PLACEMENT.

■ STITCH COUNT: THE FIRST SERIES OF NUMBERS TELLS YOU HOW MANY SQUARES WIDE AND HIGH THE CHARTED DESIGN IS. (WHEN A FRENCH KNOT FALLS ON THE EDGE OF A DESIGN, A SQUARE IS ADDED TO THE COUNT.) THEN, THE SIZE OF THE FINISHED PROJECT IS GIVEN FOR DIFFERENT FABRIC COUNTS.

LET'S STITCH!

TEACHING PIECE: FOLLOW THESE STEP-BY-STE
INSTRUCTIONS, AND SOON YOU'LL HAVE A COMPLETED
STITCHED PIECE!

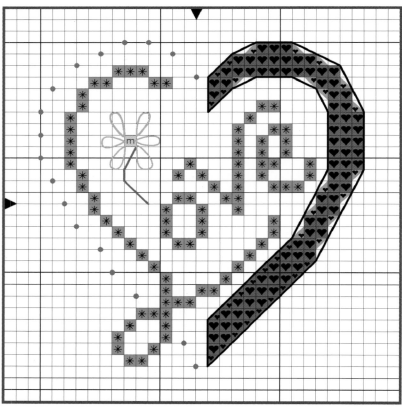

LOVE

X	DMC	¼X	¾X	B'ST	ANC.	COLOR
m	444				290	yellow
♥	606	◢	◢	◢	334	red
	907			◢	255	green
✳	3845				1089	blue
●	606				334	red French Knot
⃠	970				316	orange Lazy Daisy

Love was stitched on an 8" x 8¼" piece of 14 count Whi
Aida (design size 2" x 2¼"). Three strands of floss were
used for Cross Stitch, two strands for Lazy Daisy Stitch
and one strand for Backstitch and French Knots.

Stitch Count (28w x 30h)

14 count	2"	x 2¼"
16 count	1¾"	x 2"
18 count	1½"	x 1¾"

FOR THIS PROJECT, WORK THE STITCHES IN THIS ORDER:

1) BLUE CROSS STITCHES
2) RED CROSS STITCHES, ¼, AND ¾ STITCHES
3) YELLOW CROSS STITCH
4) RED AND GREEN BACKSTITCH
5) RED FRENCH KNOTS
6) ORANGE LAZY DAISY STITCHES

WHERE TO START

1 CUT THE FABRIC USING THE MEASUREMENTS IN THE DESIGN INFORMATION (REFER TO PAGE 6), AND THEN PREPARE THE FABRIC ACCORDING TO PAGE 2.

2 USE THE ARROWS ON THE CHART TO FIND THE CENTER OF THE DESIGN. LOCATE THE CENTER OF THE FABRIC BY FOLDING IT IN HALF, LEFT TO RIGHT AND AGAIN BOTTOM TO TOP. TO FIND YOUR STARTING POINT, COUNT THE NUMBER OF SQUARES (STITCHES) FROM THE CENTER OF THE CHART TO THE UPPERMOST LEFT FULL CROSS STITCH. THEN, FROM THE FABRIC'S CENTER, FIND THIS SAME STARTING POINT BY COUNTING OUT THE SAME NUMBER OF SQUARES (STITCHES).

3 THREAD YOUR NEEDLE WITH THREE 18"-LONG STRANDS OF BLUE FLOSS. TYING A KNOT IN THE END OF YOUR FLOSS WILL CAUSE YOUR FINISHED PIECE TO HAVE LUMPS UNDERNEATH. INSTEAD, BRING THE NEEDLE UP THROUGH THE HOLE AT 1 (SEE # 4 BELOW). PULL THE FLOSS THROUGH THE HOLE BUT LEAVE A 1" TAIL ON THE BACK. WITH YOUR FINGER, HOLD THE TAIL AGAINST THE BACK OF THE FABRIC. THIS TAIL WILL BE HELD IN PLACE UNDER THE FIRST FEW STITCHES YOU WORK. END YOUR FLOSS BY RUNNING UNDER SEVERAL STITCHES ON THE BACK.

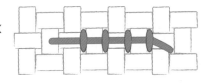

back of fabric

NOW YOU'RE READY TO START STITCHING THE BLUE STITCHES

FOR THIS DESIGN, FOLLOW THE LOVE CHART ON PAGE 6 AND WORK ALL THE BLUE CROSS STITCHES FIRST (THERE ARE NO $^1/_4$ OR $^3/_4$ BLUE STITCHES IN THE DESIGN).

4 BEGIN WITH THE TOP ROW OF BLUE STITCHES. TO WORK CROSS STITCHES IN A HORIZONTAL ROW, WORK LEFT TO RIGHT, BRINGING THE NEEDLE UP AT 1 AND TAKING IT DOWN AT 2. CONTINUE COMING UP AT 1 AND DOWN AT 2 UNTIL YOU HAVE THE NUMBER OF STITCHES IN THAT ROW. TO COMPLETE THE STITCHES, WORK BACK ACROSS THE ROW. BRING THE NEEDLE UP AT 3 AND DOWN AT 4 UNTIL ALL THE STITCHES HAVE BEEN CROSSED. AFTER YOU HAVE COMPLETED THE TOP ROW, COUNT DOWN TO BEGIN THE NEXT ROW. **NOTE: IT'S IMPORTANT THAT THE TOP STITCH ON ALL CROSS STITCHES CROSS IN THE SAME DIRECTION.**

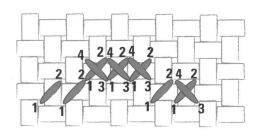 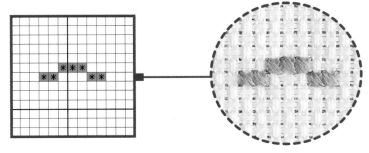

IT'S OK TO CARRY YOUR FLOSS ON THE BACK OF THE FABRIC TO AN AREA A FEW STITCHES AWAY.
BUT IF IT'S MORE THAN 3-4, FINISH OFF THE FLOSS LENGTH AND START IN THE NEW AREA.

5

CONTINUE COUNTING TO FIND YOUR STITCH PLACEMENT. TO WORK STITCHES IN A VERTICAL ROW, START AT THE TOP OF THE ROW AND BRING THE NEEDLE UP AT 1 AND TAKE IT DOWN AT 2. THEN BRING THE NEEDLE UP AT 3 AND TAKE IT DOWN AT 4. CONTINUE STITCHING THIS WAY UNTIL ALL THE BLUE STITCHES ARE COMPLETED.

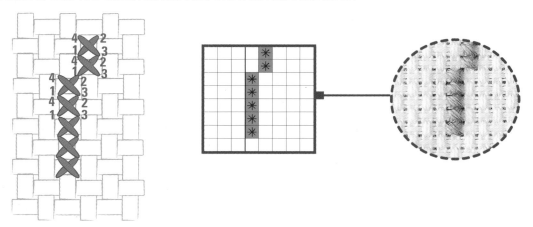

NOW YOU'RE READY TO STITCH THE RED STITCHES

THIS COLOR HAS FULL CROSS STITCHES, $1/4$ STITCHES, AND $3/4$ STITCHES. YOU WILL WORK ALL OF THESE AS YOU COME TO THEM IN THE CHART. THE $1/4$ AND $3/4$ STITCHES WILL HAVE DIFFERENT COLOR TRIANGLES ON THE CHART TO MAKE IT EASY TO TELL THE DIFFERENCE.

6

STARTING WITH THE TOP ROW, THE FIRST STITCH YOU WILL WORK IS A $3/4$ STITCH. COME UP AT 1 AND GO DOWN AT 2 IN THE CENTER OF THE SQUARE BY USING THE TIP OF THE NEEDLE TO MAKE A HOLE BETWEEN THE FABRIC THREADS; THEN, COME UP AT 3 AND DOWN AT 4. THEN WORK ACROSS THE ROW WITH THREE FULL CROSS STITCHES, WORK THE $3/4$ STITCH, AND COME BACK ACROSS TO COMPLETE THE ROW. THE SECOND ROW STARTS WITH A $1/4$ STITCH. A ONE-QUARTER STITCH IS SIMPLY ONE QUARTER OF A CROSS STITCH. BRING THE NEEDLE UP AT 1; THEN, TAKE THE NEEDLE DOWN AT 2 BY USING THE TIP OF THE NEEDLE TO MAKE A HOLE BETWEEN THE FABRIC THREADS. CONTINUE TO FOLLOW THE CHART WORKING ALL THE RED STITCHES AS INDICATED. THE $1/4$ STITCHES LOOK A LITTLE ODD HANGING OUT THERE BUT THE NEXT STEP TAKES CARE OF THAT. READ ON!

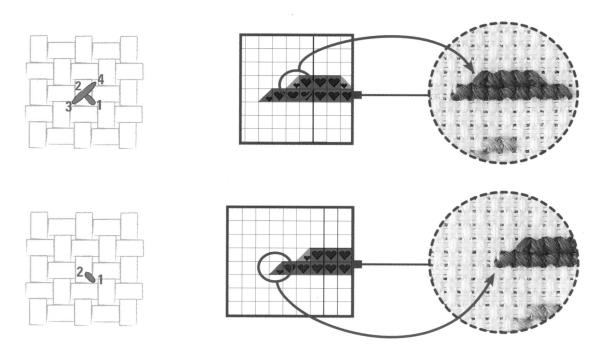

YOU'RE ALMOST FINISHED!

7 BACKSTITCH IS USED TO OUTLINE AND ADD DETAIL TO A DESIGN AND IS ADDED AFTER THE CROSS STITCHES AND QUARTER STITCHES HAVE ALL BEEN WORKED USING ONE STRAND OF FLOSS. COME UP AT 1 AND ALL **ODD** NUMBERS, AND GO DOWN AT 2 AND ALL **EVEN** NUMBERS. CONTINUE UNTIL BACKSTITCHING IS COMPLETE.

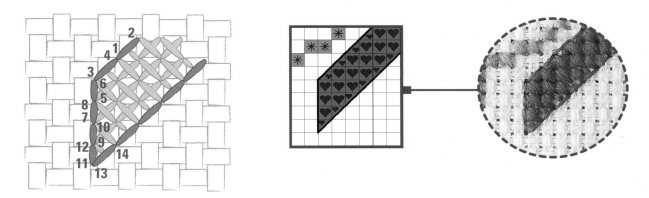

8 FOR FRENCH KNOTS, USING **1** STRAND OF FLOSS, BRING THE NEEDLE UP AT **1**. WRAP THE FLOSS ONCE AROUND THE NEEDLE. OE AT 2, TIGHTEN THE KNOT, AND PULL THE NEEDLE THROUGH THE FABRIC, HOLDING THE FLOSS UNTIL IT MUST BE RELEASED. FOR A LARGER KNOT, USE MORE FLOSS STRANDS AND WRAP ONLY ONCE.

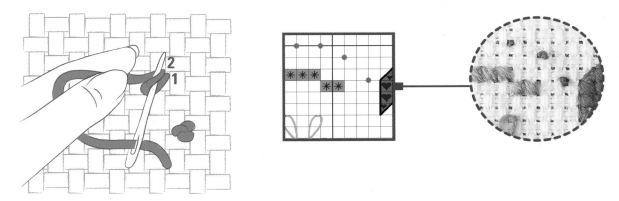

9 FOR LAZY DAISY STITCHES, BRING THE NEEDLE UP AT **1** AND MAKE A LOOP. GO DOWN AT **2** AND COME UP AT **3**, KEEPING THE FLOSS BELOW THE POINT OF THE NEEDLE. PULL THE NEEDLE THROUGH AND GO DOWN AT **4** TO ANCHOR THE LOOP, COMPLETING THE STITCH.

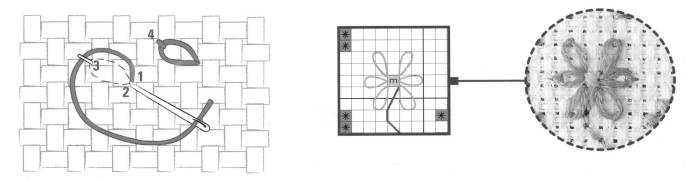

CONGRATULATIONS! NOW YOU KNOW IT ALL!

STITCH AT A GLANCE

FOLLOW THE STITCH DIAGRAMS TO BRING THE NEEDLE UP AT ODD NUMBERS AND DOWN AT EVEN NUMBERS.

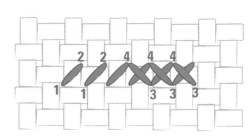

CROSS STITCH IN A HORIZONTAL ROW

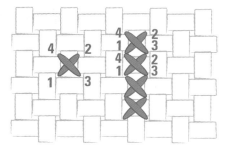

CROSS STITCH IN A VERTICAL ROW

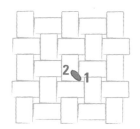

ONE-QUARTER STITCH

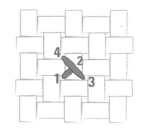

THREE-QUARTER STITCH

HALF CROSS STITCH

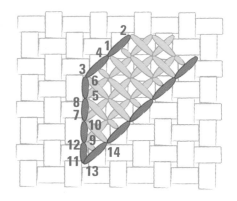

BACKSTITCH

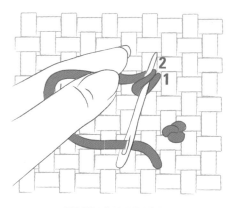

FRENCH KNOT

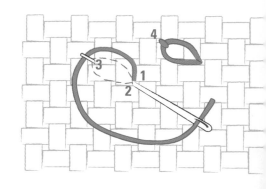

LAZY DAISY STITCH

FLOSS: BUY ALL THE FLOSS FOR YOUR PROJECT AT ONE TIME TO ENSURE IT IS FROM THE SAME DYE LOT. DIFFERENT DYE LOTS MAY HAVE SLIGHT COLOR VARIATIONS WHICH MIGHT NOT SHOW UP WHEN HELD TOGETHER, BUT ARE APPARENT ON A STITCHED PIECE.

IT'S ALL ABOUT THE DETAILS!

STITCHING ON LINEN

UNLIKE EVENWEAVE FABRICS, CROSS STITCH ON LINEN IS GENERALLY WORKED OVER TWO FABRIC THREADS. FOR EXAMPLE, STITCHING ON **28** COUNT LINEN OVER TWO THREADS IS THE SAME AS STITCHING ON **14** COUNT AIDA. THE STITCHES SHOULD BE PLACED SO THAT VERTICAL FABRIC THREADS SUPPORT EACH STITCH. MAKE SURE THAT THE FIRST CROSS STITCH IS PLACED ON THE FABRIC WITH STITCH **1-2** BEGINNING AND ENDING WHERE A VERTICAL FABRIC THREAD CROSSES OVER A HORIZONTAL FABRIC THREAD.

THE PROJECTS SHOWN ON PAGES **22-23** WERE STITCHED ON LINEN.

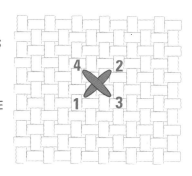

ADDING BEADS

MANY CROSS STITCH DESIGNS USE BEADS TO ADD DIMENSION AND SHINE. TO ATTACH BEADS, USE ONE STRAND OF FLOSS AND A FINE NEEDLE THAT WILL PASS THROUGH THE BEAD. SECURE THE FLOSS ON THE BACK OF THE FABRIC. BRING THE NEEDLE UP AT **1**; THEN, RUN THE NEEDLE THROUGH THE BEAD AND DOWN AT **2**. SECURE THE FLOSS ON THE BACK OR CONTINUE TO THE NEXT BEAD.

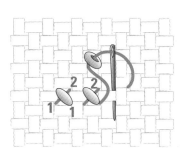

FRAMING

SO, YOUR COMPLETED DESIGN WON'T FIT IN A PURCHASED FRAME AND YOU DON'T WANT TO ORDER A CUSTOM-MADE FRAME? USE A PURCHASED FRAME THAT IS THE CLOSEST FIT AND HAVE A MAT CUSTOM CUT.

FLOSS

EMBROIDERY FLOSS CAN BE FOUND IN EVERY IMAGINABLE COLOR INCLUDING METALLICS, VARIEGATED COLORS, AND OVER-DYED THREADS.

NOW, DO SOMETHING WITH ALL THAT COOL NEW CROSS STITCH KNOW-HOW!

LOOK AT THE DESIGNS IN THE PROJECT GALLERY. PICK ONE YOU LOVE AND GET STITCHIN'!

STAMP 'N STITCH

THE STAMP 'N STITCH TECHNIQUE IS SO SIMPLE, YET PRODUCES SUCH FANTASTIC, ONE-OF-A-KIND RESULTS IN A VERY SHORT PERIOD OF TIME. SEE A STEP-BY-STEP STAMP 'N STITCH DEMONSTRATION WEBCAST AT WWW.LEISUREARTS.COM.

STAMP 'N STITCH INSTRUCTIONS

YOU ONLY NEED: A COUPLE OF STAMPS, SOME INK, A PIECE OF CROSS STITCH FABRIC, EMBROIDERY FLOSS, MASKING TAPE, STAMP CLEANER, AN OLD TOWEL, AND A RULER.

YOUR STAMP 'N STITCH DESIGN BE WILL ONE OF A KIND. CHOOSE A STAMP (OR SEVERAL STAMPS) THAT REFLECT YOUR PERSONALITY, YOUR DÉCOR, AND THE WORD YOU HAVE CHOSEN TO STITCH.

CHOOSE INK COLORS THAT COORDINATE WITH YOUR EMBROIDERY FLOSS. YOU CAN USE THE FLOSS COLOR(S) GIVEN YOU IN THE COLOR KEY(S) OR CHOOSE YOUR OWN. BOTH PIGMENT AND DYE INKS WILL WORK WHEN STAMPING ON FABRIC, BUT PIGMENT INK PADS ARE "JUICIER" SO YOU'LL GET MORE INK ON THE STAMP AND A STRONGER IMAGE ON THE FABRIC.

TEST YOUR STAMPS AND INK COLORS ON SCRAP AIDA OR LINEN TO BE SURE YOU LIKE THE COLOR(S) AND EFFECT.

STAMPS CAN BE RUBBER, ACRYLIC, OR FOAM. SOME VERY DETAILED STAMPS PRODUCE BEAUTIFUL RESULTS; OTHERS ARE TOO FINE AND LOSE DETAIL WHEN STAMPED ON FABRIC. THE LARGE FOAM STAMPS THAT ARE AVAILABLE FOR CHILDREN AND STAMPING ON WALLS ARE GREAT FOR BACKGROUND COVERAGE.

STAMPING TECHNIQUES

BASIC STAMPING: APPLY INK AND PRESS THE STAMP ONTO THE FABRIC IN THE DESIRED AREA. DO NOT ROCK THE STAMP; APPLY DOWNWARD PRESSURE. LIFT THE STAMP OFF THE FABRIC. RE-INKING BEFORE EACH APPLICATION, STAMP ADDITIONAL IMAGES UNTIL YOU ARE SATISFIED WITH YOUR DESIGN.

OVERSTAMPING: OVERSTAMPING IS THE SIMPLE PROCESS OF STAMPING A DIFFERENT DESIGN IN A DIFFERENT COLOR OVER WHAT HAS ALREADY BEEN STAMPED.

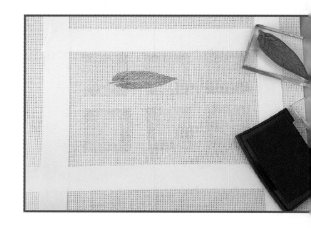

FINISHING TOUCHES

YOUR STAMPS WILL LAST FOR MANY YEARS IF YOU CLEAN THEM AFTER EACH USE. CLEAN STAMPS WITH STAMP CLEANER AND A TOWEL.

ONCE YOUR DESIGN IS STAMPED, ALLOW THE INK TO DRY AND REMOVE THE TAPE. STITCH YOUR DESIGN WITHIN THE STAMPED AREA, BEING CAREFUL TO KEEP THE FABRIC CLEAN AND AS UNWRINKLED AS POSSIBLE. DO NOT WASH THE FABRIC AFTER YOU HAVE FINISHED STITCHING; THE INK MAY RUN. INSTEAD, TURN THE FABRIC TO THE WRONG SIDE, SPRITZ WITH WATER, AND PRESS. PLACING A TERRY TOWEL ON THE IRONING BOARD BEFORE PRESSING THE STITCHED PIECE PREVENTS STITCHES FROM BEING FLATTENED.

E STAMP 'N STITCH TECHNIQUE
PRESENTS THE BEST OF BOTH WORLDS:
QUICK-FINISH PROJECT THAT TRULY
FLECTS YOUR PERSONALITY. JUST
BBER-STAMP THE DESIGN OF YOUR
OICE BEFORE CROSS STITCHING.

AMP 'N STITCH STEP-BY-STEP
STRUCTIONS ARE ON PAGE **12**.

IART AND FINISHING DETAILS ARE ON
GE **38**.

STAMP 'N STITCH
REFLECT

STITCH 'N PAINT

THE STITCH 'N PAINT TECHNIQUE USES BACKSTITCH AND WATERCOLOR PAINT ON CROSS STITCH FABRIC TO GIVE YOU ALL THE DETAIL OF CROSS STITCH IN A FRACTION OF THE TIME. BEGIN BY BACKSTITCHING YOUR DESIGN AND THEN FOLLOW THESE EASY INSTRUCTIONS TO ADD WATERCOLOR PAINT. YOU CAN VIEW A WEBCAST DEMONSTRATION OF THIS TECHNIQUE ON OUR WEB SITE, WWW.LEISUREARTS.COM.

STITCH 'N PAINT INSTRUCTIONS

YOU WILL NEED:

AIDA FABRIC WITH BACKSTITCHED DESIGN
SCRAP AIDA FABRIC FOR COLOR TESTING
WHITE PAPER TOWELS
PAINT PALETTE

FREEZER PAPER OR WAX PAPER
PAINTBRUSHES OF VARIOUS SIZES
CRAYOLA® WATERCOLOR PAINTS
SMALL BOWLS OF WATER

ASSEMBLE YOUR SUPPLIES. USE A SCRAP OF AIDA FABRIC LARGE ENOUGH TO TEST PAINT COLORS AND TO ALLOW YOU TO PRACTICE APPLYING THE PAINT. IT IS IMPORTANT TO USE WHITE PAPER TOWELS, AS THE COLOR FROM A PRINTED PAPER TOWEL COULD BLEED ONTO THE FABRIC. WE USED A WHITE FOAM PLATE FOR A PAINT PALETTE.

PROTECT THE WORK SURFACE WITH WAX PAPER. PLACE A PAPER TOWEL UNDER THE STITCHED DESIGN. SINCE YOU WILL NOT BE ABLE TO WASH THE PAINTED DESIGN, TRY TO KEEP THE FABRIC AS CLEAN AND UNWRINKLED AS POSSIBLE WHILE PAINTING.

WET A PAINTBRUSH AND APPLY WATER TO THE DESIRED PAINT COLOR UNTIL IT IS A CREAMY CONSISTENCY. USING THE PAINTBRUSH LIKE A SPOON, TRANSFER PAINT ONTO THE PALETTE. RINSE AND BLOT THE BRUSH. USE A DAMP BRUSH TO TEST THE PAINT COLOR ON A SCRAP PIECE OF AIDA.

IT MAY SOMETIMES BE NECESSARY TO BLEND PAINT COLORS TO GET THE DESIRED SHADE. BE SURE TO MIX ENOUGH COLOR TO PAINT THE ENTIRE AREA.

TO APPLY PAINT TO THE STITCHED PIECE, BEGIN AT THE CENTER OF THE AREA YOU'RE PAINTING AND PUSH THE PAINT TOWARD THE BACKSTITCHED OUTLINE.

ONCE THE DESIGN IS PAINTED, ALLOW THE PAINT TO DRY. USE A DRY IRON TO PRESS THE DESIGN FROM THE WRONG SIDE.

TIPS:

- IF THE APPLIED PAINT COLOR IS TOO VIBRANT OR TOO DARK, QUICKLY BLOT THE PAINT WITH A PAPER TOWEL AND MOST OF THE COLOR WILL BE LIFTED FROM THE FABRIC.

- IF YOU WISH TO DARKEN A PAINT COLOR AFTER YOU HAVE PAINTED YOUR PIECE, SIMPLY ADD A SECOND COAT OF PAINT AFTER THE FIRST HAS DRIED. IF YOU ADD MORE PAINT TO AN AREA WHICH IS STILL WET, YOU RUN THE RISK OF THE PAINT BLEEDING OUTSIDE THE STITCHED LINES.

THE STITCH 'N PAINT TECHNIQUE IS
ANOTHER WAY TO FINISH YOUR PROJECT
IN A HURRY. JUST BACKSTITCH THE
DESIGN AND FILL IN THE COLORS WITH
CHILDREN'S WATERCOLORS.

STITCH 'N PAINT STEP-BY-STEP
DIRECTIONS ARE ON PAGE 14.

CHART AND FINISHING DETAILS ARE ON
PAGE 39.

STITCH 'N PAINT
GARDEN

SHOW OFF YOUR NEW STITCHING SKILLS
WITH THIS TRADITIONAL CROSS STITCH
SAMPLER—EVEN IF YOUR DWELLING
PLACE ISN'T ALL THAT HUMBLE.

CHART AND FINISHING DETAILS ARE ON
PAGES 28-29.

PLANT HUMILITY

BECAUSE WE ALL KNOW FOLKS WHO
EMBRACE NONCONFORMITY, WE OFFER
THE SAME DESIGN WITH AN UNEXPECTED
SENTIMENT.

CHART AND FINISHING DETAILS ARE ON
PAGES 28-29.

I WANT IT ALL

BACKSTITCH-ONLY BIRD STITCHED ON
SEAFOAM GREEN FABRIC IS QUICK,
CLEAN, AND MODERN.

CHART AND FINISHING DETAILS ARE ON
PAGE 30.

ON THE WING

...THEY WOULDN'T CALL IT WORK, AND
...OU WOULDN'T HAVE TO BE THERE. BUT
...NCE YOU DO, WHY NOT LIGHTEN THINGS
...P WITH THE THOUGHT THAT'S ON
...VERYONE'S MIND?

...HART AND FINISHING DETAILS ARE ON
...AGE 27.

...E'RE ALSO GIVING YOU THE ENTIRE
...LPHABET, SO YOU CAN GET ALL THOSE
...EELINGS OFF YOUR CHEST.

...LPHABET CHARTS ARE ON PAGES
...5-26.

ALPHABET

FRUITS, VEGETABLES, AND HERBS
SAMPLER IN UPDATED COLORS FOR
THE BUSY COOK IN YOUR HOUSE
— WHOEVER HE IS.

CHART AND FINISHING DETAILS ARE ON
PAGES **32-33**.

FRENCH MARKET

ITCH THE BLOSSOMS IN THE LOWER
ALF OF THIS DESIGN, THE BACKGROUND
THE UPPER. IT'S A GRAPHIC ARTS-
SPIRED APPROACH TO THE TRADITIONAL
ORAL CROSS STITCH.

HART AND FINISHING DETAILS ARE ON
GE **34**.

BLOOMING GRAPHIC

JUST A QUICK ROW OF FULL CROSS
STITCHES, TWO LINES OF BACKSTITCH
AND A FLORAL ICON TO FRAME A
SNAPSHOT OR BORDER A MONOGRAM.

CHART AND FINISHING DETAILS ARE ON
PAGE 35.

ARTS AND CRAFTS
BORDER

WE LOVE THE IDEA OF THE SILHOUETTE IN COLOR, ESPECIALLY THESE COLORS.

CHART AND FINISHING DETAILS ARE ON PAGES 36-37.

BIRDS

WE LOVE THE LOOK OF THESE 1910-ERA TIMES NEW ROMAN NUMERALS, ALL STACKED IN REGIMENTED ROWS.

CHART AND FINISHING DETAILS ARE ON PAGE 31.

NUMBERS GAME

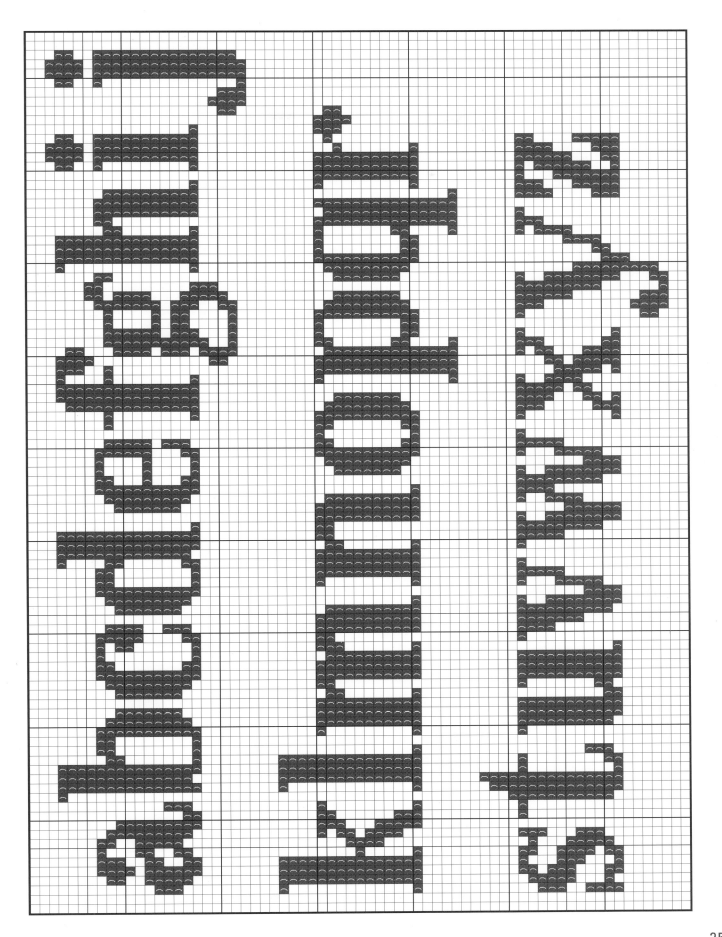

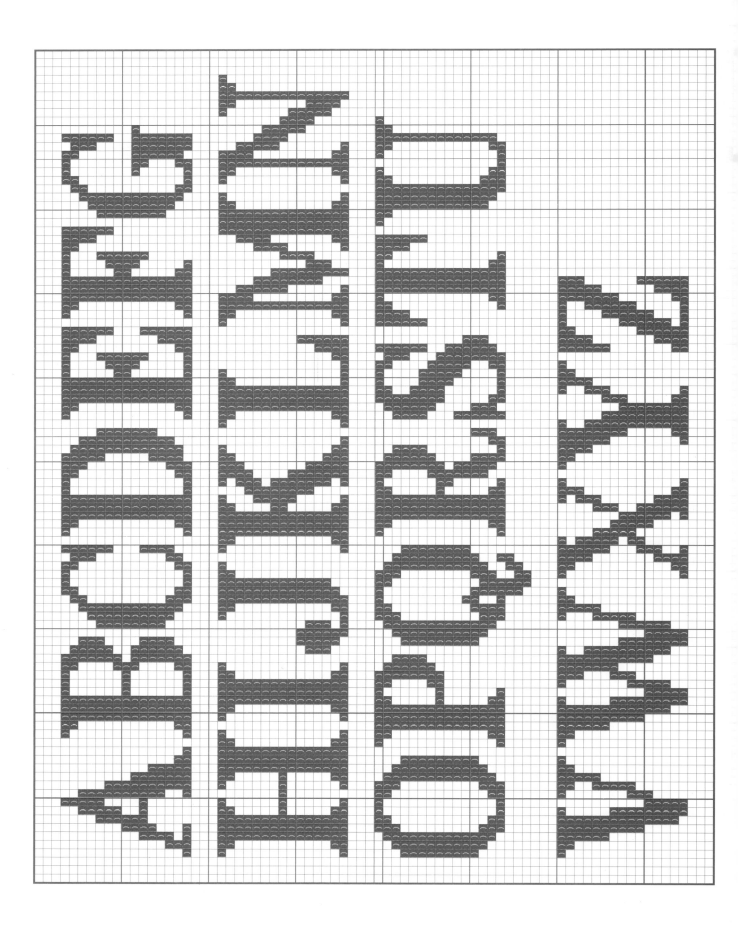

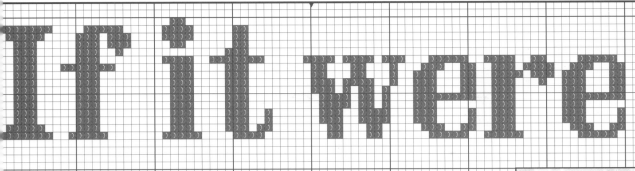

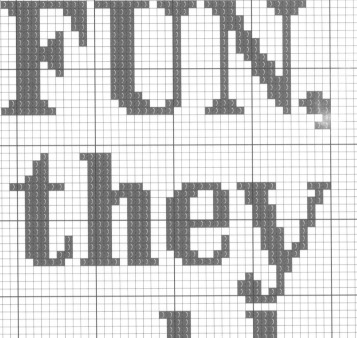

X	DMC	ANC.	COLOR
❯	310	403	black

Alphabet was stitched on an 11¾" x 14½" piece of 14 count White Aida (design size 5¾" x 8½"). Three strands of floss were used for Cross Stitch. It was inserted in an 8" x 10" frame.

Stitch Count (80w x 117h)

14 count	5¾"	x	8½"
16 count	5"	x	7½"
18 count	4½"	x	6½"

PLANT HUMILITY

I WANT IT ALL

X	DMC	ANC.	COLOR
☆	ecru	387	ecru
a	420	374	brown
✕	729	890	gold
#	935	861	dk avocado
◇	3051	681	avocado

X	DMC	ANC.	COLOR
+	3052	262	lt avocado
L	3768	779	blue
♥	3777	1015	terra cotta
◢	3787	273	gray
⊥	3830	5975	dk terra cotta

Plant Humility and **I Want It All** were each stitched on an 11" x 11" piece of 14 count Natural Aida (design size 5" x 5"). Three strands of floss were used for Cross Stitch. **Plant Humility** was framed using a 9" square frame. **I Want It All** was framed using a 17" square frame and a custom cut mat with a 5¾" opening.

Design by Diane Williams.

Stitch Count (67w x 67h)

14 count	5"	x	5"
16 count	4¼"	x	4¼"
18 count	3¾"	x	3¾"

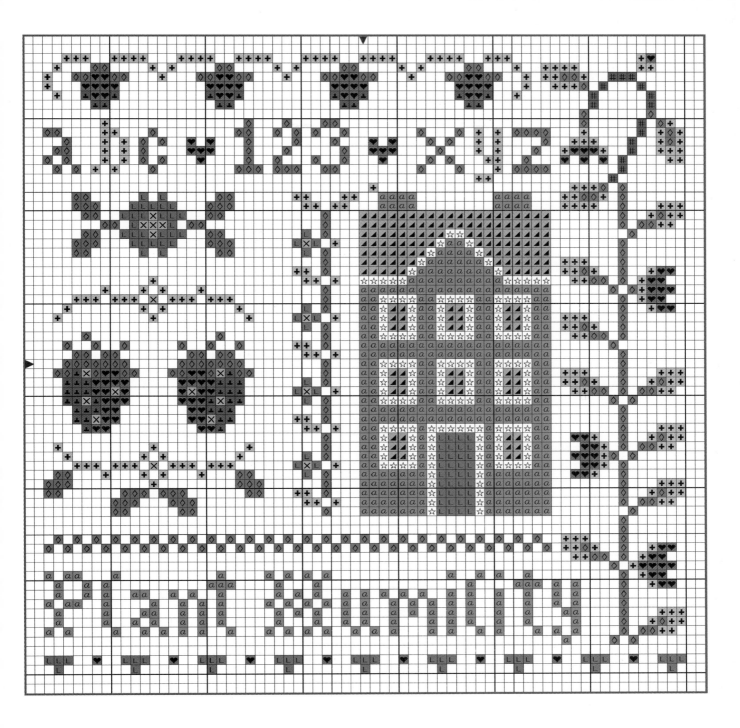

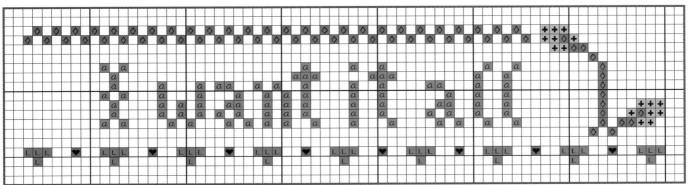

ON THE WING

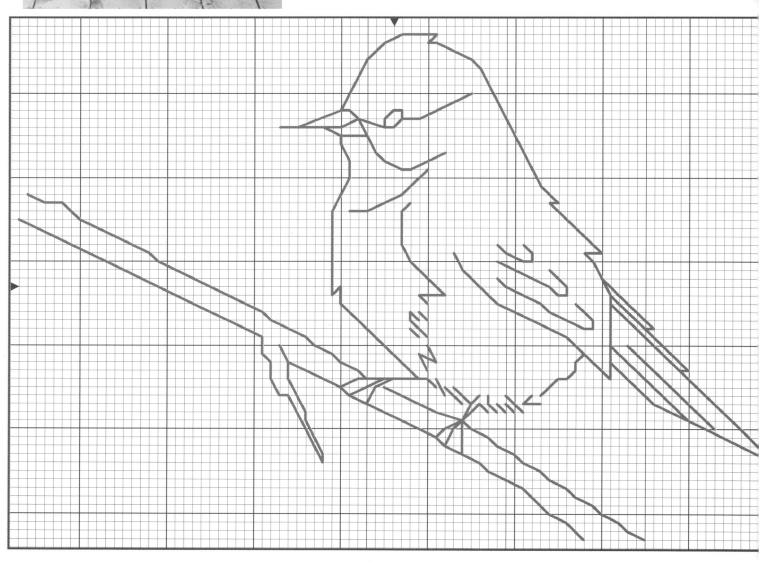

X	DMC	B'ST	ANC.	COLOR
	3814	⊡	1074	green

On the Wing was stitched on a 12¼" x 10½" piece of 14 count Light Seafoam Aida (design size 6¼" x 4½"). Two strands of floss were used for Backstitch. It was framed using an 11" x 14" frame and a custom cut mat with a 5" x 7" opening.

Stitch Count (86w x 60h)

14 count	6¼"	x	4½"
16 count	5½"	x	3¾"
18 count	5"	x	3½"

NUMBERS GAME

X	DMC	¼X	¾X	B'ST	ANC.	COLOR
☒	3021	◩	◩	╱	905	brown

Numbers Game was stitched on a 10" x 11½" piece of 14 count Ivory Aida (design size 4" x 5½"). Three strands of floss were used for Cross Stitch and one strand for Backstitch. It was custom framed using an 8" x 10" frame and a custom cut mat with a 4¾" x 6¼" opening.

Stitch Count (53w x 74h)

14 count	4"	x	5½"
16 count	3½"	x	4¾"
18 count	3"	x	4¼"

FRENCH MARKET

X	DMC	¼X	B'ST	ANC.	COLOR
7	154	7			dk purple
◣	315	◣		1019	dk mauve
a	316			1017	mauve
♥	347	◢		1025	dk salmon
◢	349	◢		13	dk coral
#	350	#		11	coral
m	351	m		10	lt coral
⊠	471	x		266	avocado green
8	472			253	lt avocado green
*	580	*		281	green
+	581	+		280	lt green
◆	597	◢		1064	turquoise
∨	712	v		926	cream
+	747	+		158	blue
L	772	L		259	lt yellow green
3	817	◢		13	red
✖	869	x		944	brown
	898		╱	360	dk brown
5	3328			1024	salmon
(	3348	(		264	yellow green
C	3823	c		386	lt yellow
↑	3834	◢		100	purple
H	3835			98	lt purple
☆	3865			2	white
●	898			360	dk brown French Knot

Grey area indicates last row of previous section of design.

French Market was stitched on an 11¾" x 11¾" piece of 14 count White Aida (design size 5¾" x 5¾"). Three strands of floss were used for Cross Stitch and one strand for Backstitch and French Knots. It was custom framed using a 12¾" square frame and a custom cut mat with a 6⅛" square opening.

Design by Polly Carbonari.

Stitch Count (79w x 79h)

14 count	5¾"	x	5¾"
16 count	5"	x	5"
18 count	4½"	x	4½"

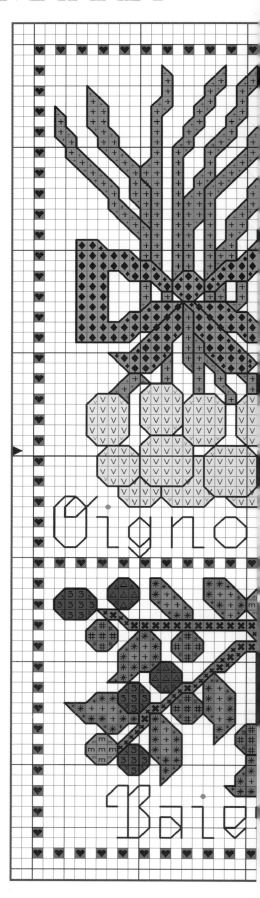

Radis Raisins

aubergines

pruneaux

Basile

BLOOMING GRAPHIC

X	DMC	¼X	¾X	B'ST	ANC.	COLOR
▲	471			✏	266	green
8	720	8	8	✏	326	dk orange
a	722			✏	323	orange
♥	817	♥		✏	13	red
H	938	H	H	✏	381	brown
+	3855	+	+		311	gold

Blooming Graphic was stitched on a 9¾" x 9¾" piece of 14 count White Aida (design size 3¾" x 3¾"). Three strands of floss were used for Cross Stitch and one strand for Backstitch. It was custom framed using a 12" square frame and a custom cut mat with a 4¾" square opening.

Stitch Count (50w x 5		
14 count	3¾"	x
16 count	3¼"	x
18 count	3"	x

ARTS AND CRAFTS BORDER

X	DMC	¼X	¾X	B'ST	ANC.	COLOR
✖	3371	◣	◢	╱	382	brown

Arts and Crafts Border
was stitched on a 10¼" x 12¼"
piece of 28 count Dirty Cashel
Linen (design size 4¼" x 6¼")
over two fabric threads
(see page 11 about working
on Linen). Three strands of
floss were used for Cross Stitch
and one strand for Backstitch.
It was framed using an 8" x 10"
frame and a mat with a
5" x 7" opening. Photo was
affixed to the linen using
photo corners.

Stitch Count (58w x 86h)

14 count	4¼"	x 6¼"
16 count	3¾"	x 5½"
18 count	3¼"	x 5"

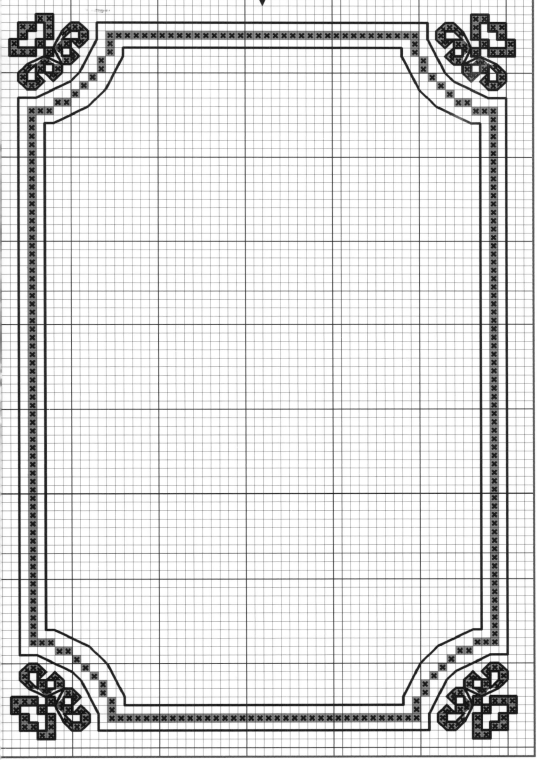

BIRDS

X	DMC	¼X	¾X	B'ST	ANC.	COLOR
▼	839	◤	�￩	╱	1086	brown
✕	3816	◣	◲	╱	876	dk green
▲	3817	◣	◲	╱	875	green
＋	3862	◣	◲	╱	358	lt brown

Birds was stitched on a 12¾" x 10¾" piece of 28 count Light Sand Cashel Linen (design size 6¾" x 4¾") over two fabric threads (see page 11 about working on Linen). Three strands of floss were used for Cross Stitch and one strand for Backstitch. It was framed using a 14" x 11" frame and a custom cut mat with a 7" x 5" opening.

Stitch Count (92w x 64h)

14 count	6¾"	x	4¾"
16 count	5¾"	x	4"
18 count	5¼"	x	3¾"

STAMP 'N STITCH
REFLECT

STAMP 'N STITCH STEP-BY-STEP INSTRUCTIONS ARE ON PAGE 12.
SEE A SHORT WEBCAST OF THIS TECHNIQUE AT WWW.LEISUREARTS.COM.

X	DMC	ANC.	COLOR
a	898	360	brown

Reflect was stitched on a 13½" x 14¼" piece of 14 count
Ivory Aida (finished design size, including stamping, 7½" x 5¼").
Three strands of floss were used for Cross Stitch. It was custom framed using a 13" x 11" frame.

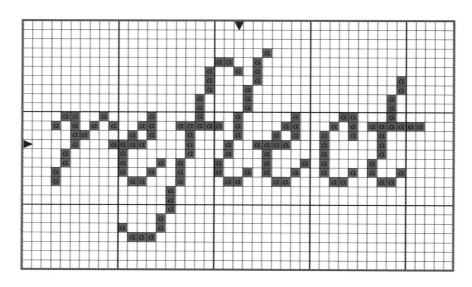

Stitch Count (39w x 21h)

14 count	3"	x	1½"
16 count	2½"	x	1½"
18 count	2¼"	x	1¼"

STITCH 'N PAINT
GARDEN

STITCH 'N PAINT STEP-BY-STEP INSTRUCTIONS ARE ON PAGE 14.
SEE A SHORT WEBCAST OF THIS TECHNIQUE AT WWW.LEISUREARTS.COM.

DMC	B'ST	ANC.	COLOR
938	◹	381	brown
938	⊙	381	brown French Knot

Stitch Count (87w x 60h)

14 count	6¼"	x	4½"
16 count	5½"	x	3¾"
18 count	5"	x	3½"

...arden was stitched on a 12¼" x 10½"
...ece of 14 count White Aida (design size
...¼" x 4½"). Two strands of floss were used for
...ackstitch and French Knots. It was framed
...sing a 5" x 7" frame.

THE PRODUCTION TEAM:

WRITERS: DEB MOORE & JOYCE SCOTT HARRIS

EDITORIAL WRITER: SUSAN MCMANUS JOHNSON

SENIOR GRAPHIC ARTIST: CHASKA RICHARDSON LUCAS

GRAPHIC ARTISTS: ANGELA STARK & JANIE MARIE WRIGHT

PHOTO STYLISTS: KIM KERN & CHRISTY MYERS

Instructions tested and photography models made by Muriel Hicks, Donna L. Overman, Angie Perryman, and Patricia Vines.

Fabric provided courtesy of Charles Craft, Inc.
Embroidery floss provided courtesy of the DMC Corporation.

We have made every effort to ensure that these instructions are accurate and complete. We cannot, however, be responsible for human error, typographical mistakes, or variations in individual work.